Dear _____,

This stocking stuffer is especially for you! Don't forget to send Santa Claus your wish list for Christmas. Remember, Santa is watching to see if you're naughty or nice! Very soon Santa is coming to town!

Yours truly,
St. Nicholas

St. Nicholas
Special Delivery

North Pole
Coloring Book

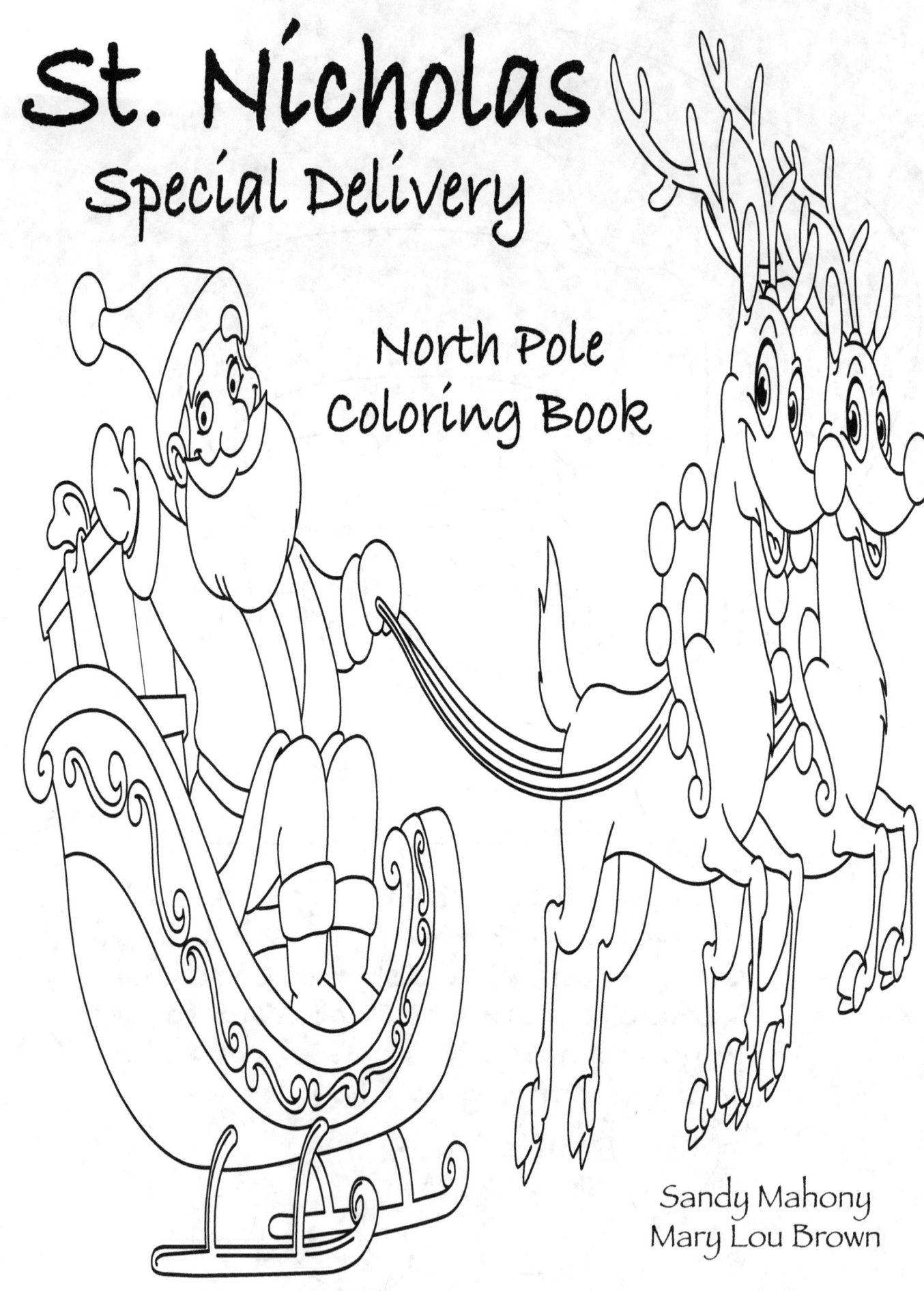

Sandy Mahony
Mary Lou Brown

January 2016
OFFICE OF EVALUATIONS AND SPECIAL PROJECTS

OIG HIGHLIGHTS

View Report

Evaluation of the Department of State's FOIA Processes for Requests Involving the Office of the Secretary

What OIG Reviewed

As part of ongoing efforts to respond to requests from the current Secretary of State and several Members of Congress, the Office of Inspector General (OIG) evaluated efforts undertaken by the Department of State (Department) to ensure that records are properly produced in response to Freedom of Information Act (FOIA) requests involving past and current Secretaries of State. This report addresses (1) the Department's compliance with FOIA statutory and regulatory requirements and (2) the effectiveness of the processes used by the Office of the Secretary's Executive Secretariat (S/ES) to respond to FOIA requests.

What OIG Recommends

OIG recommends that the Bureau of Administration identify personnel needed to improve the timeliness of FOIA responses and to quickly acquire those resources.

OIG recommends further that the Department develop a quality assurance plan to identify and address vulnerabilities in the FOIA process.

OIG also makes two recommendations to S/ES to ensure that its FOIA searches are complete and accurate.

Based on the Department's responses to a draft of this report, OIG considers all of these recommendations to be resolved, pending further action.

What OIG Found

S/ES is responsible for coordinating searches for FOIA requests for records held by the Office of the Secretary. When a FOIA request of that nature is received by the Department, the Office of Information Programs and Services (IPS) within the Bureau of Administration notifies S/ES. S/ES reports its findings to IPS, which then communicates with the FOIA requester.

OIG's past and current work demonstrates that Department leadership has not played a meaningful role in overseeing or reviewing the quality of FOIA responses. The searches performed by S/ES do not consistently meet statutory and regulatory requirements for completeness and rarely meet requirements for timeliness. S/ES currently searches Department email accounts only if a FOIA request mentions emails or asks for "all records," or if S/ES is requested to do so during the course of litigation. However, FOIA and Department guidance require searching email accounts when relevant records are likely maintained in these accounts. In addition, although FOIA requires agencies to respond to requests within 20 working days, some requests involving the Office of the Secretary have taken more than 500 days to process. These delays are due, in part, to the Department's insufficient provision of personnel to IPS to handle its caseload.

These problems are compounded by the fact that S/ES FOIA responses are sometimes inaccurate. Officials in IPS and attorneys for the Department identified instances in which S/ES reported that records did not exist, even though it was later revealed that such records did exist. Procedural weaknesses in S/ES FOIA processes appear to be contributing to these deficiencies. For example, S/ES management is not monitoring search results for accuracy, and IPS has limited ability to conduct oversight. S/ES also lacks written policies and procedures for responding to FOIA requests. Finally, staff in S/ES and other components in the Office of the Secretary have not taken training offered by IPS to better understand their FOIA responsibilities.

In September 2015, the Department appointed a Transparency Coordinator to improve the Department's FOIA process, among other things.

_____ Office of Inspector General _____

U.S. Department of State • Broadcasting Board of Governors

Office of Inspector General

ESP-16-01   Office of Evaluations and Special Projects   January 2016

Evaluation of the Department of State's FOIA Processes for Requests Involving the Office of the Secretary